The Oval Hou

Winner of the Iowa Poetry Prize

Poems by **Kathleen** *Peirce*

The Oval Hour

University of Iowa Press Iowa City

University of Iowa Press, Iowa City 52242
Printed in the United States of America
Design by Richard Hendel
http://www.uiowa.edu/~uipress
Printed on acid-free paper

Library of Congress Cataloging-in-Publication Data
Peirce, Kathleen, 1956–
The oval hour: poems / by Kathleen Peirce.
p. cm. (Iowa poetry prize)
ISBN 0-87745-664-x (pbk.)
I. Title. II. Series.
PS3566.E34O83 1999
811'.54—dc21   98-44842

99 00 01 02 03 P 5 4 3 2 1

FOR LOUISE FRANCES PEIRCE

Contents

Acknowledgments

Grateful acknowledgment is made to the following publications, in which some of the poems in this book first appeared:

Antioch Review
"Two Sisters"

The Best American Poetry, 1994
"Divided Touch, Divided Color"

Colorado Review
"Divided Touch, Divided Color," "Round," "Dyke Breach," "Confession 1.8.13," "Confession 7.5.7," "Confession 9.4.10," "Confession 9.10.25," "Confession 11.11.13," and "Confession 8.9.21"

Field
"Expulsion and Annunciation," "Wren," "Thought Might Nod in Waves," and "Person, Place, Gesture, Thing"

Ohio Review
"Grace"

Paris Review
"Five-Part Question," "Nearness and Entrance," "Figure with Trees," "Mother and Son," "The Many Colors," "Confession 11.23.29," "Confession 10.8.13," "Nude against the Light,"

"Mountain Laurel," "Of the Veritable Ocean," "Ovidian," and "Homage to the Romantic Ballet"

Texas Observer
"Mirror Forest" and "Thimble Forest"

Windhover Press, Iowa City, published a limited edition collection in 1995 titled *Divided Touch, Divided Color* in which the following poems appear: "Figure with Trees," "Pygmalion in March," "Self-Portrait as Landscape," "Mother and Son," "Grief," "Divided Touch, Divided Color," and "Taking Pleasure."

My gratitude as well to the Mrs. Giles Whiting Foundation in New York and the Sewall Elam Foundation in Austin for their generous support.

The Oval Hour

Ovidian

Who stares into a wood and sees a dress fastened to a tree
recalls the torso of a man with arms held up among the wrens
and desires the man. Who moves among desires understands
stasis is the harder art. What feels like one is often two,
as how eyes look, or more than two, as how sunset opposes
noon, or how desire abides in memory, roving where
a girl in woods unfastens her sundress, a tree suspends
a flock, wrens flutter in a girl, a torso gently aches
inside a tree. The eye wants something other than it sees,
and what it sees. A hem lifts in the leaves.

Days and nights of the most and largest changes
in her tenth year. Absolute time had always been near,
but in that year it entered her seemingly
by letting go either end. Why would a child think
of what she was before?
During the days, place stayed constant, house
of her whole life, where she knew every thing
in every drawer and cupboard. Why wonder
what anything becomes?
The days made room according to the light.
She would be on a cot in the breezeway, her body
on the body of the cot, in the body of the breezeway,
being and not waiting.
It was a green meshwork as much as the woods were,
or the cottonwood letting fly its fairy princesses.
Some thing would be in her hand, the white but scratched
skin of the birch she'd peeled, or ruffles from the overblown
peony. She knew fragrance as a kind of voice.
Nights were bodiless. Crickets turned from form and were
their sounds. Think of her turning off the bathroom light
to hurry the feeling on, happy to make the tub unknowable
through whiteness, happy that water can become its farther
part, removed from clarity and sparkling.
She is of a size that can float there. But
when she opens her body and slides forward, time enters
in a vibrancy and changes her, and leaves her this
pleasure now, later desire.

Confession 1.8.13

Passing through innocence, I came either to experience
or guilt, or they came to me, displacing innocence,
which didn't leave (where would it have gone),
and yet it was no more. I was no longer
an unmarked girl but a woman gesturing.
It was not that the world showed itself to me
in a set method. Longing in stillnesses
and various tendencies of thought, I thought to be touched
by the world as it willed, or by whoever knew me.
I did myself, by the understandings objects gave me,
practice this touching, this being touched.
When things said themselves, and saying, sang,
I listened and imagined they themselves were presences
of stillnesses and movements, a music visible.
That they meant themselves and no others was plain
from shapes they took as leaves or men or rain. And so
by my constant thoughts on shapes as they appeared,
I collected what they stood for, and having broken in
my body to these signs, I gave gestures of opening to it.

Nude against the Light

You for whom the day was sad, among you
there were some whose days are never
otherwise. Among them, there were very few
whose presence shone despair so violent
we hated them. They said
the angels at the feeder are dying as they sing,
they said a painting demonstrates failure to see
the portion of a woman not created with brush strokes,
regardless of the brightness of the room. The room
is bright. So much so that, broken down, the light,
having passed through lace, cut there
by the order of a loveliness particular
and rare, magnifies the objects of the room,
brings them to supplication, to being as a rendering
of surfaces the eye is helpless to resist, there being
so much pleasure in that place. The figure's nakedness is drawn
to be included as a surface but resists, as she is other than
a wovenness, a carved thing, painted thing. She was not
made by hand. Neither is she only made of how or where
she looks, as sunshine seems to be. She
regards herself. Or she's diffused, already entered
the seizure of daylight on coverlet and wall, taken by a heaven
of negligible outlines. If this is so, the figure separate from light
must be our memory of her. She was so sad, who found each pleasure
better than herself, and irresistible.

Confession 10.8.13

Collect and recollect. These things I do
within, where, present with me is the world
and whatever I could think of it,
and what I have forgotten. Some things
I buried, though they seemed self-buried,
or slipped out of my mind when they had
glided further into me as I believed
them gone. Once my mouth had been aroused
by the side of a man's thumb moving over it,
the image fixed in me by that impress
recalls the hand, or my heightening,
as if I know my lover when I have him,
or when I have no one. In this way
my mind contains my body and can keep
in mind delight, whether I revisit with the
pleasure of my body, or I revisit thinking
my sad thoughts, or I keep back my desire
like the broken animals.

Confession 4.2.3

In hope of loving what is real
and in hope of being loved
by something real, believing that my mind
is intermingled with what is done by me,
what is the seeing of a snake in the rope
except hallucination, and what else is the seeing
of a deer on the path when there is
no deer there? When I feed the wind
with thinking and longing, am I the pleasure
of nothing? I have not seen a vivid wind,
and trying caused my eyes to close
and I saw nothing, no differently
than when I fall asleep. Mornings I know
the mirror that reflects my face
reflected first its maker as all mirrors do,
and returns me a reversal of myself.
How will I recognize the secret shapes
of my accompaniment, and what word would I say?

You who were perfectly simple and true
as we were simple and true (except that we were
flesh, and the breaths that left us passed
and never came again), you who didn't change,
you who never deceived, waking or dreaming,
while we slept and woke beside a trellis of clematis
shaking with the implications of mannered withering,
or woke beside a river that had killed itself for love,
you pure sign among the beautiful women,
you who hung the same between sisters
as between the mothers and girls,
you, dressed as the cleft between the letters
of any written word, visible and blank and absolute,
the final wave, the mouthed word from the eldest daughters
boarding trains for modeling school
forced a weary, historic sadness to emerge.
When we asked, the less learned among us answered
they did not know you; the more learned never did.

Pygmalion in March

This world is not human. In my loneliness the spirea
kept close to the house while the distances took white.
Tender and supple, dead looking, by resemblance it coaxed me
to imagine the tops of the catalpa and the oak
where no hands go, where god is.
When the last snow fell with rain and disappeared,
pricking the white field so the mud broke through,
I kept sitting at the window.
Forked, sparrow colored, crossing and recrossing,
the spirea showed me how a shape can't help but touch itself.
Then I knew god to be a shapelessness
overseeing form. When even the smallest twigs began
distending smallest ivory buds, it was then I remembered
memory and saw the shrub as it was going to be,
heavy with the dusty-smelling white flesh of itself. Briefly,
briefly, the shape and the idea of the shape filled the image full.
Like a god, against my disappearing, I invented her.

Evening Poem

If the coronal suture of the young deer's skull
is the smallest trough for listening for death, it begins

or ends, weak or tentative, behind the eye and equals
or approximates the wavy track a mole delineates

along a cemetery fence at dusk. *Going home*, we think.
The maddening or ecstatic thinness of such lines

delights and mortifies those talking there, who see each other
oddly banked by mounds of plastic flowers, and further,

deeper, amid lovers who made, finally, families in shrouds.
She thought to bring a candle. He thinks to whorl

its changeful surface with his singular fingertip, or he does it
without thinking. Would that he could imprint,

as on a correspondence fixed with sealing wax, only
love's evidence, labyrinth, and alphabet.

Two Sisters

There they are before desire went to them,
one preferring spring, when the smaller shapes
seem really willing to be seen, one preferring fall
for the yellow heaviness dragging over over-ripeness,
opening it before it leaves. These two are children.
One knows to sleep on top the other, fitting her cheek
against her thigh with a turned-out head,
knees hooked over the farther thigh, a ladle and tureen.
From her shoulders to her hips the smaller body crosses
her sister's open legs. The larger one has looked
at how she's crossed to magnify the feeling, and she'll
look again. She loves the spring. Her sister floats under
the arm draped over her and the cupped hand roving
her sleepy sleepy head where something opens and
divides and illustrates, divides and wants reverberation,
wants the floaty feeling after being touched by form,
then formlessness. She loves the fall.

Figure with Trees

One shoulder breaking the tension of a satin slip,
making the strap fall loose inside the dress.
Bend of the gesture sliding the strap back, into place,
one frond of the mimosa.

Something hurts her. Or, head bent, she's sleeping
sitting up. Heavy beauty in the curved, lax hands,
two gold bracelets crossed. But her knees have fallen
open under the stitched cloth, and her mouth has. Red
edge of one ear, red five-petaled hand. The one shoulder
brought outside the bodice of the dress.

Wind is a kind of looking, different in a cedar
than a sycamore. Hundreds of cedar on this hill. Rare sycamore,
common wind. Four pretty mimosa.
Her human shoulder moving when she breathes.

Thimble Forest

Finite, the emplacement of eight thimbles
on eight upright pins. Then the shutting of the lid
forever over them. The eye-hole was merciful,
but the human hand shakes so, bringing pleasure on,
that the thimbles quivered with me when I looked in at them,
but when none fell I didn't want to be their leitmotif
and I removed myself as if immortal,
but having seen, I feel them waiting to be seen.

Mirror Forest

Vertical junipers whose heads pitch
out of reach. A blue sky, then a black sky
never or always touching them. Love makes for itself
precarious foundations. Like wind moves,
I feel you moving over me, while the trees appear
moved through. I understand that to look into a mirror
is not to enter it. I saw the way the one tree leaning over moving water
moved like water, I saw the surfaces refracting like my words.

Seahorse Forest

Armless, legless, clinging to. How I have been
required to still myself with the filigree
I am made of. I had held one frond near ground
until I thought the frond resembled me.
Then I was visited, and though my other
rarely faces me, I sensed we were equine
and rare, small to view among the fathoms
but unbroken, perpetual, and our own.

What is the joy of the moral heart
if the great secret of morals is love,
if my heart, trying its nature,
makes a mirror of itself
for a body not my own,
if my heart is returned to me
as a body of water will return a face
without sensing its accomplishment, water
so different in the final armslength
of daylight, seeming to soften as it darkens
but really only darkening after all, and even then
my mirror bent over the evening water,
the voice of objects saying *love what*
refuses you and the voice of heaven saying
praise your correspondence with all things
beautiful there below, and my own voice
assigned to ask *O behold my heart.*

Jessamine

The morning is dark and wet as if darkness and wetness
had been done to it, had undone the common chipperness
of what there had been to expect. Shall we be relieved?
Not only is the little yellow flower softer for it,
it lasts longer, and water moves slantwise off and on between,
and because between, among all outside things. Why shouldn't I
want to think of wine asleep in casks with my eyes closed?
Wasn't this always with me, the serene pause in things
held back from touch? How is it the weather feels
to have turned from what things want?
What should I let inscribe itself onto me as you do,
who love me all you can and not enough?

Of the Veritable Ocean

There was no sea for her to sing beyond the genius of,
but she had heard of it, and knew a version
where a blue, a grey, a foam moved, very grand
between two horizontal stillnesses, not toward,
or for, or of her, she who was too small
to go outside alone. Nor was it actual
sea, but seawater adhering to a gulf. Between her body
and the water were trees where someone had attached so many
oranges. Why, and how?

There never was a sea, but in time there was a view,
a hill she learned to listen from, and she seemed most moved
by other people talking. One said *the caves I carve with my mass*
echo some great songs I do not recognize. This was spoken
as a lake of tears would speak. Another said *you want me more*
than I want you. One sobbed forth a sentence that he knew
would instigate his vanishing against his will. There was
no sea, but after certain sentences some silences
were like the genius of a place she could become

if not a song, an open mouth followed by swallowing,
self-aroused as waves seem self-aroused without the presence of
a moon, or like fragrance increasing with a rose's helplessness.
This was her strength. There was no sea. Its absence
meant the world to her, as she was not

required to sing, nor did she claim a listener.
She required a world, or a version of a world
intense enough to overwhelm in times when
not much happens, where an orange is orange, and
full with being touched by other waters.

Grief

The same woman passes on my sidewalk.
She leaves me every day.
Here is her walking stick with bells strapped on,
odd in a plain way, the safest simplest things
strange merely by their happening at once,
as through a neighbor's window a lace is seen
occurring on a horsehair davenport. Or one detached
white flower in the yard, trumpet shaped, enough for one hand,
an exquisite drinking thing made of cup and mouth,
what love is until you look away, until you see a whole catalpa tree
heaving off these flowers by the thousands, meaning grief.

Mother and Son

When his arms raise it's all he knows of how
a body opens. Light and full,
his body in the moment just before she touches him
knows to meet and fill the contours of the day, so that her
hands, cupping his sides, duplicate his sides
to make him twice contained. He is not less
when she lets go because the day receives him
with brief obedience in ways too various to count,
if he could count; daylight rakes the barrier
she's put him on, a cemetery wall, with striped giddiness.
Cars passing make the darker stripes, and stripes of sound.
He can't tell if he finds things or they come to him.
If he looks farther on, the narrowing wall seems pulled out of itself,
so he looks where he stands. Pebbles make the wall's top
lion colored. Pale upright stones align in the interior,
a field for the greater presences: calm blue hydrangea,
angel with made hands, wings, and face held out,
stuck in radiance. These worlds are shapely and occasional
as she is now, who lifts him down.

In my village (*comus*) there is a song (*oda*),
a comedy no one remembers the inception of,
though our elderly weep, remembering
the diminished voices of their elders
growing in weakness, serenading them,
whose voices are diminished now.
Our song is matter without form
set into our children, an almost-nothing,
like the filament the spider fastens to the branch
that sets a leaf to twirl rather than fall;
we sing with thought, but not the *is, is-not*
which is thought's origin. When we sing, we cease to be
what we have been, and begin to be what we were not,
whether we sing while acting out the obligations
of our days, or, with devotion, sing
to the lovers in our beds, for we began in hell.
Our song (*oda*) is of the goats (*tragus*).
We sing to praise our will to murder them.

Red

Reason in the hummingbird feeder:
it's what they're drawn to. They themselves
shall not be red but some have red, banded
at the throat and only in some light.
Their lives are beautiful
but their endings sad; their lives are sad
but their endings beautiful.
Some days it appears that things are stilled
in a cascade of possibilities, and it seems
important that the table not be moved
any farther into the body of the room, as when
lying on the floor just looking at its underside
was more appropriate when you were a child,
and that the low, wide, flat, black bowl stay empty
except for the false chase of fishes stamped into its rim,
and that the bowl be at the center of the table. Unless
you were really thinking of it, it would not occur
that the rim could have been said to be a lip.

Wren

The house wren had more beauty on a sad day.
Someone thought of himself as sitting without thinking.
He would have said neither was there feeling.
The feeder hung where he'd hung it,
and he'd filled it. Why be ashamed?
Moments that seemed not to make the morning
crossed the morning and he wondered
what he'd had before that thought occurred to him.
Less? A making ready? Why would his mind
make arrangements toward a desire he didn't know?
The painted bird sprang down and ate,
random and consequential.

Confession 7.5.7

And when I asked where evil is
sometimes I asked in evil ways
and so was blinded to the evil
in my search. When what is particular
seemed small (the fuchsia zinnia,
dog's tooth, rain, a man asking me
to look away from him) I was corrupted
by belief that she who asks to be increased
is made safe by the courage of her question.
But when I recognized (by my revisiting)
the meeting place of the particular
and the immense, evil was strange to me,
the colors of the flowers vast,
the dog's tooth more wet than the rain,
and I became obedient, and looked away,
against no one, having learned to fear
my will (overequipped for measurement),
and came to love what kept itself from me.

Expulsion and Annunciation

Holding the fruit against her ribs, she looks despondent.
He isn't touching her. Let's untie that twine of her fingers
from the model of charity. We have the chirp
of crickets in December in the South. Do you think
or is there a ceiling under which the heavens roll?
Above the depth and breadth and height of her desire
there was only more desire, his three fingers
and her body moving on them. Here and now, it's only
thinking moving on thought, trill and chirp
into which enters one dog's ecstatic, cone-shaped
bark, like thought put into you.

Dyke Breach

Anything in the extreme.
Oh how different difference is,
how resistant to easiness, wordplay, and everyday-
ness. How unlike everything everything is when we are
there. Field of poppies to the left of the road.
Put there, but that hardly matters. Did the packages
of seed say red? Pure red, pure joy? Rapture
is a word not with us anymore but hysteria is.
Break me down says the extreme thing,
laughing and sobbing. The third pure poppy is a red
unlike the second, unlike the first. The field,
the field, the field is more than everything,
us out of the car now, another painter getting the paintbrush
away from himself, flinging it or ignoring it, reaching
for the spatula and red, putting it there, which means
everything finally, smearing it, the two figures
red where they stand, intense (in tension) (intention),
making us want to bring our bodies there. It's for
afterwards, it's all for the look-away,
the whatever-it-is we see we have after.

Confession 11.19.25

God to whom nothing new will come,
I am a bonnet covering a rose,
and at my end I will be completely world,
or I am a drum with death inside,
waiting for a mandolin. My son
is a parrot carrying a ladder
to his future where a woman in a boat
smiles from among her hundred flowers,
or he is a soldier with a vase inside,
waiting for a spider. You for whom sensation
is perceivable, oversee the making of his
sexual bed, his dream bed, death bed.
Induce his unfolding, imperceptible to you,
imperceptible to you to whom nothing
new will come, while I continue singing
of the realm of things he might believe
in a world of arriving and vanishing.

Butterfly House

From the foyer, the corner of the waterfall fell
behind the portion of the glass wall that contained it.
We could see parts, and we could only see.
The day was in there, irreducible even though
made to come into a box of glass. Of the giant fronds
and leaves and stems and blooms, none needed us.
We were withheld, outside but not outdoors.
Did the moment's indentation come bulging
out at us or were we pressing in, what with
us and the grand room dense with such interiors,
and which was more accompanied, more occupied
by that pair whose outsized wings kept them at our height,
or were they only heavy or giddy about how alike they were
and are, azure number one and azure number two,
hemmed with black, accentuated, operatic really
in their mutual intent to play the beloved's voyeur
until death and in midair, though what's midair
under a roof? Ours was an emergency in the most
emergent sense, some words floating out from the head
of one of us toward the other's head and in,
in slow-time, then the other's turn,
ruminating on perfection in eternity.

None live without death,
but I have believed along with those
who believe in dying in one's sleep,
as if sleep is a cutaway of presence where
loss can be felt less, as though I had forgotten
vividness called forward in my sleep (flowers
too red, the stairwell narrowing),
or I had not watched, excluded and enamored,
the sleep of those I love. Given my body,
either I live slow of heart and have the world
magnified and exterior to me, and lick the shadows
of things seen and the temporal, or I live
to receive and rehearse vividness,
inwardly kissed by the eternal internal of
everything, or I pretend to be untouched
and whole and satiate, forgetting that sweetness which
is ripeness also is decay, and in each way come to know
death, and am furious with death.

Dreaming All Night

A man goes walking away from his house,
down a long road in the rain. It feels
wonderful to him. Down and down he walks and comes to
a creek and he stops, watching the water move fast
then faster in front of him, and the creek widens
and hurries more, and widens, and he steps back
and is amazed. A boat floats by. Just as he sees it
he reaches out and grabs the lanyard and he pulls it in.
He gets in and lies down, and the rain is
dropping on his face, and the boat is moving in the current of
the water, and when he looks the sky is moving, too. This lasts
so long the boat fills up with water, which he doesn't realize
until the water starts getting in his mouth. He sits up.
The creek that was a stream is now a lake, and widening, but the boat
bumps into land, and he gets out. He walks onto an island,
and above him are leaves of every green dripping and dripping. He
walks by flowers, all kinds of flowers of all colors closed up
waiting for the sun. He walks by. The rain is lessening. The grade
of the path he walks on is getting steeper, but so gradually that he
barely recognizes it. The overgrowth ends and he steps out of it
and things have changed. The rain has stopped, and before him
in the distance is his house. He walks there, walks inside, and there
are his wife and child at the table, eating supper. She looks at his
shoes and he does, too. Look at that mud, she says, but he sees
gold. It's gold, he says. Look. Where have you been, she wants to know.
I was walking. Look at you, she says.

Confession 3.10.18

Of the times I felt myself an ornament
of the world, it was always with the clarity
of my body moving over a larger body,
brought to move as a bracelet rolls upward on the arm
when the hand, without consciousness,
is lifted to the eye or mouth, or as a bracelet falls
to its limit when the arm swings down,
the wearer made aware, pleased by having been so
added to. But if the world had been aware of me,
and had been given pleasure by my moving over it,
I would have known, the way a lover knows the other's arm
as an adornment greater than the silver at its wrist,
and the rock that generates a stone daylight can pass through
would have been obvious to me, and the memory of flowers
exhaled by the interior of the fig would have been as the aperture
a child's body, a man's body could pass through,
and I would have asked for equal mercy
for myself and fragrances.

The Dead

Might they really want to let go of giving back?
Let's not let them, who do they think
they are. Before the first death,
there was a horse even a child could see
grazing in an important way among
the headstones. It was the white color of rescue,
and it was hungry. Also there was a nut-sized
piece of brown stained glass with milk in it
broken from the mausoleum door.
Even a child would remember the air
coming out that hole as an abstraction.
If that dreamy heavy horse and that dry air
were not hers, she knew they wanted to be
thought of anyway. They stay awake in her.

Promesa

He will not take fire in his hands
because his hands are fire. When
he prays, sudden birdsong
transmogrifies the bladed places
fire makes of itself into an expectation
for retort. All failures move this way,
though one is left with, if alone, a sight
for images. Songbird on a brown-
black branch among the ochre-
charcoal atmospheres. Burnt sienna,
pitch. Tan and jet. Sparrow, for whom
do you sing other than your likenesses?

Homage to the Romantic Ballet

From the pyracantha in November, fire-berries hang
and burn. The inference that abundance weighs one down
is a thought made by fearing, though the branch's orange-red
    bedecking
signals it. Please, could we realize today that our thinking is ascribed,
as the median grasses realize themselves as pinkish brown,
formerly beautiful in green, but less beautiful before today. It may be
we have these thoughts because we love each other,
striking continually as we do against and into present time,
one prevailing wind countering another with a branch in between,
or an unobstructed breeze overtaken by a gust,
a whiff rolled over by a puff, or a simple sigh let go
across another's lower back with only the involuntary tensing
of a muscle in response. How unused we are
to sensing proof that being helplessly extends itself,
except for the awareness of continuous desire.
The room containing the first sleep of love
is cold, and waves are heard arriving constantly,
leaving shells outside to recognize as wings or bones,
and fish bones that resemble feathers. It is the duty of all lovers
to forecast the pearly cadences of every inner thing, even though
the beach describes the apprehension every woman ages with,
that the supreme interior requires vanishing.
Sentences wave; waves bear and set the mollusks down;
one arranges to be lived in by another.

Thought Might Nod in Waves

The gentle, curvy tendrils of wisteria won't
make leaves until I tie them to the post.
What's waiting worth? Thinking can live there:
smoke in the mind before the cigarette's lit,
thought of wetness making wet
or not; thought might nod in waves
unattached, unattached, as with the half-fear
in reading so often how he hurts her,
how she hurts him, seeing it on a screen,
light opening a room with no one in it
yet. So, when the half-pink, papery, spent body
of the bougainvillea flower was let go and hit me
I was made ready and knew to make my fear noise.

Edenic

Fire, but a fire barely discernible
from the blue atmosphere containing it,
held not by a rendering of will alone,
or desire alone, but a desire comprised of will
embedded in an ecstasy just able to contain itself.
Fire as god, blue atmosphere as fear of god.
Fire as body, blue the benevolence
required to sustain it. One clothed, the other undressed.
Each wondering this far and no further? Words form,
part of the snake ever in the mouth. One says to the other
can I kiss you there. Time passes, parts pass across
parts. Yes or no, both wonder. Then and afterward.

Pietà

In the place of death and so as not to die of the other's death,
there is a place of wakefulness where shapes take shape
according to light brightening, passing colors out,
a place of sleep according to light darkening,
retrieving them, a place of death where the faintest exhalation
holds interiors and atmospheres and the gladiolus
opens in succession from the inmost out.
I am without my other, imagining the beautiful
as objects will me to. You, new voice opening near at hand,
will you, if I will, speak until my own death comes?

Because I cannot understand how things are made,
I seek to be perfected, to watch myself being made,
fluttering between the motions
of things past and to come, as if presence
is not possible in present time
except between the hands of *was* and *going to be*,
and not like between hands, but like between
the motions of the hands. My first food was the body
of my mother, and though I have no memory
of eating there, should I believe that her movements
have lasted me? Or when a man brings to my mouth
food he has prepared for me, should I resist
the understanding of the uninvented future offering?
A long time becomes long by motions passing by. Eternity
is still. What should being be?
What have the bodies of the others to do with me?
What did my hand do? What did my mouth
bring about? What will it bring about?

Confession 11.23.29

My mouth brings loss to me
as it takes measurement of being,
as I think how far, how deep,
how many, how much more,
drawing sentience in always as a double inhalation
of the known and what there might be to expect.
A mirror pressed against a mirror makes
a locked infinity, a bliss ruined by entering,
an anti-kiss. When my mouth opens
against another human mouth,
I measure whirlings of an object on a wheel
which stops (whether or not I pause,
or if I am slow, or quick with love, or twice as quick).
And then I speak of time, and time,
and times, and times, and come to know
loss, so vehemently kindled toward
love, and the mouth of love
which draws away from me.

Person, Place, Gesture, Thing

Woman with a book unopened.
Place where the bleeding heart bloomed last year.
Her lighting a cigarette making him hard.
Stair step to trip on.

Man singing in his mind only.
Room closed on two asleep.
Heavy picture pulling on the nail.
Fork in a drawer.

2

His beautiful body, his brother's suicide.
Dark in one room, dark in the next.
Her laugh unwinding with the horse's whinnying.
Pinecones that crackle as if to each other.

Her face in the dream, the sumac reddening.
Under the bed, above the bed, under the house, above.
Staining the garment, staining the whole life.
Whole body of time.

3

Woman with a book unopened.
Man singing in his mind only.
His beautiful body, his brother's suicide.
Her face in the dream, the sumac reddening.

Place where the bleeding heart bloomed last year.
Room closed on two asleep.
Dark in one room, dark in the next.
Under the bed, above the bed, under the house, above.

Her lighting a cigarette making him hard.
Heavy picture pulling on the nail.
Her laugh unwinding with the horse's whinnying.
Staining the garment, staining the whole life.

Stair step to trip on.
Fork in a drawer.
Pinecones that crackle as if to each other.
Whole body of time.

Five-Part Question

I saw the upholstery guard clamped on the back
of the seat in front of me.

I saw my own body the usual way, frontal
and from the chest down, facing the empty chair.

I saw three moving pictures: one out the window,
one the window itself, and one the whole car rocking.
The scene outside moved through the moving window,
and the window moved inside the train,
but the train moved by itself.

I saw thinking hiccup from an actual memory
of a true train to a thing I'd only thought about:
tunnel vision. Thank god it wasn't in the world outside.
It was in the aisle of the train.

I saw its inhabitant. It was you, honey, *and* your body.
O delicate and curious, can you guess what I remember
that I thought I dreamed you want?

Round

Half-light under the vaulted dome of the gymnasium.
The group moves ovally. In this weather,
both light and dark are true. The eye
sees or not, the mind praised less
by less illuminated things. The bodies make
and keep a time, but separately, as a thought contained
and not contained.

                What can come in, in this hour
with and without light? Two keep circling,
offering their backs. One is multiple,
a clot of soldiers in green-brown synchronicity,
and a woman keeping strange time, jogging while she braids
and unbraids her brown hair. Beauty is repulsive if
it's touched too much, but in this light, this loss of light,
each is met by equal portions of its opposite;
fingers crabbing through her blowzy hair are somehow
sweetened by her gait, sweetly pigeon-toed.

                      Her waiting boy,
so bored with his body, five years old, so bored with the room,
bored with the raw trees circling the day,
meets with revelation: a simple seeing
of the wall clock: five till four. He can tell,
finally, time. His knowing feels to have been
waiting all along. Now the bodies pass, and cross
his thought. Sound the feet make. Feel
of the clock. His sound everybody's sound.

A Trade

If the geranium could lay hold of
one moment of sensation as though holding one
memory of a prior morning
with a friend licking rainwater from its red face,

someone could be simple and vivid
and miraculously draw the small and
deeper beauties upward to compose a face
enough to ask the other come.

Divided Touch, Divided Color

—Georges Seurat

As soon as I walked out I felt the mistake in the weather,
how the lesser light on the droplets hanging and flying
off the yew's bough had fooled me into readiness
for a chill. It was a Tuesday. I'd made my note on the yew berries,
how beautifully distinct from green they are, even in minimal light.
What satisfying clusters! Seeing one, one seeks another,
and the tree responds easily in particles nearly rational,
or rationally assigned: the range of blues grouped beneath a smaller
    range
of grays, and then one sees the tree. Forgive me. I hesitate to tell
how frightened my little walk made me. It was a Tuesday,
the day my father comes. I wore the scarf and gloves.
In the graveyard I feel calmer, but the oaks had been changed, opened,
emptied since the last time by one rain. I saw they had become a line
    of cries,
and felt them filling me before my mind could think. Then the crow
    flocks
circled and fell in, binding every opening along the topmost edge
in a shrieking charcoal line, a line trying to enclose a shape and failing,
making the eye curl around. Someone, thinking of snow, had placed
    a toy
on every child's grave. That night, Signac came for dinner, shocked
by father juggling the knives, one of which he screws into the false end
of his arm. In my plate I see a painting of a plate. In my wife,
a jar of powder. My father is a black line eating snow.

Confession 9.10.25

What would grief be softened by
except the company of newer loss,
what can the body do but enter
and be entered, if not by the mouth
of love, by words from mouths that made
love possible, or by the memory of words.
What's spoken stops. No body can be entered
without stopping, but thoughts on voices want
that. Shhh, he said, holding down my arm
so he could brush the wrist again. If
the flesh is hushed, memory ravishes,
stands under loss, stupefied by understanding,
marries absence to desire, both being outside of time,
and makes a riddle of similitude. Behold the corpses
carried to the burials. That page is blank.
What was said into me and done with me
I stay held for, as when the honeyed bodies
overtook the rooms.

First Lines

He opens her. She can't have him.
She can't have him but he opens her.
He opens her because she can't have him.
She can't have him until he opens her.
He opens her until she can't have him.
She can't have him while he opens her.
He opens her, regretful she can't have him.
She can't have him regretful when he opens her.

Riddles

He opens her. She can't have him.
Day following night.
She can't have him but he opens her.
Clay and water.
He opens her because she can't have him.
Hive in a tree.
She can't have him until he opens her.
Peony and ant.
He opens her until she can't have him.
Wind in grass.
She can't have him while he opens her.
Cloud and rain.
He opens her, regretful she can't have him.
Phrase and mockingbird.
She can't have him regretful when he opens her.
Root and weak branch.

Poem in Summer

After the tension of heaven,
it would feel good not to be overseen,
to imagine the most beautiful heads of marigolds
as minds flaunting an after-afterlife,
temporary again, variant, physical, confined,
unpicked. Imagine not being thought of,
being without being seen: gold
or less gold, yellow, orange-yellow, lemon,
yellow-brown. But now the zinnias seem strangely
badly dressed, and thinking so gives souls
that have outreached us their way back.

Confession 2.6.12

In the extreme of soul's creation,
what desire is absurd? If I am required
to continue speaking to your back,
I will speak to your back, for this also
gives me shape as it gives my thinking shape,
though it rounds my shoulders where
the tendons hold the body to the head,
and my head leans forward always
in a shape not beautiful in women,
while my eyes, fixed on your negligence,
mark me as your theft, and must be beautiful
if stolen. How did it begin to become good
to go untouched, when seeing made the mind
want what it loved without restraint,
when my memory of being seen suggests
I have been beautiful? If my beauty was invented
and consumed by love, if I am shaped finally
by love's abandonment, am I not shaped by love?

Personae Separatae

If I keep running down the sand hills of Morocco, I will
keep waking to the grainy constellations fallen out my ears
on the pillow in the mornings afterward. Pristine, separate,
separated, roseate, those particles first seemed to me
my sleep. Also, truly, those words describe my ears,
through which, into which, so much has passed
since last we spoke, since you spoke to me. Although a face,
as I've said many times, a face does not consist
of namable elements, when I describe the tangerines
sliced and dashed with cinnamon somehow patterned
as a star, I know you think for a minute only of my mouth,
or I hope you will, as when the professor brought along
your drawings while vacationing in France
and mailed one each week to your pallor
at the hospital, you thought of his tongue bringing on
the sealed envelopes. Thank you for writing
that the mountain laurel there are having their own way.
I remember further that those were your first drawings
of your face, that you were shy and clumsy making them,
but, delivered, they seemed a little beautiful to you. I write
in that vein. I'm learning to become accustomed to the figs. The tea
is good. In an empty beautiful hotel I was asked to choose among three
dining rooms, the blue, the green, the red. I chose the red. The days
are roseate, though now I miss a boy who passed me, walking,
four days in a row. Night separates the days. The quiet starts to close
the years. The quiet stars are close and separate as ears,
mine from each other, mine from yours.

Confession 3.2.2

In the dream, your body, having
turned away, writes down the elegy.
Its words are objects of your sense
and I grow willing to be scraped being touched
by them, though I desire first that words are made
of fictions, as if the brown leaf is the false body
of the green, or the green leaf
the false body of the tree. How much more grief
it is to think that words have souls, how much more
pleasure to love them. If words
have no souls, they would not be objects as they are,
or objects of love. They are unsafe
and slant and visible as any body interlocked,
though your body remains turned, and you write
my elegy, and my own mind made this
in a dream. The reader is not called on
to relieve, but if I relive grief inside a dream
of words, why wake unable to remember them?

Self-Portrait as Landscape

If two wild dogs come at her from the standing corn in March,
the dead leaf sounds will come inside the quiet morning,
simple as earliness inside a day. What the invisible holds,
fog blurs. Still, reason's the horizon kept on the move by her desire,
the mind's horizon linear, hilly, waving off in two directions,
punched up from underneath, tacked down. There's water hanging in
    the air.
Then there's her fear: the rushing dogs, the day, her face.
The rushing day, her face. The day a collapsible cup drunk from
    another way,
instant and different where the air inverted shows itself inside the fog,
where the day's sucked deeply inside its own smallest part,
and the quiet never leaves the shaking leaf. *One summer he nearly drowned,*
a Cree poem goes, *but he saw his face / a long time*
in that lake. / He learned his face then.
The quiet never leaves the shaking leaf. That's good,
because so much does leave. The unseen hawk whose shapes
she'd have no answer for bounds off a tree. The dogs *make*
something of her scent, then trot. The fog that held the distance off
wears thin. An incommunicable blue breaks through. How odd she is,
being here and happy.

Mountain Laurel

The women were the room and the room was full,
not of women but of cadences and bedclothes, cadences irregular
and full, as drapery rounded by a recurrence of a wind
or by sequential unrelated winds all of a night
and of bedclothes, of nightgowns, white bedclothes gone blue,
moved on by a wind, rumpled there by bodies, wind,
and night in a long generation of arrivals of nighttime,
and the nightgowns were long also, also repeated, also
blue, and the bodies of the women of the room were loose
and long and white where they had been assigned to sleep,
but they are not sleeping, they will not sleep as they have been
assigned, these several women from the South and elderly.

Amaranth

Deer come to the porch
and eat the portulaca. A thought of
its fuchsia flowers being chewed
is its own succulence. The next night
they strip the yellow rose. When I was stupid,
when I was sleeping, my own voice told me
to look up *amaranth*. A small purple flower;
also an imaginary flower that does not fade.
What in the world did I think I was, believing
I could move from one to another without death?

Confession 4.13.20

Tuesday, burning
cedar. Wednesday, rain.
Thursday, scent of either
inside both. Dry hand
the body had made wet.
Do you see I look for nothing
but indications of his love?
Is it beautiful, one invisibility
embedded in another, sailed
by what, input exactly where?
It attracts without being asked,
though it has been assigned
as I have been assigned, marked
by being elsewhere earlier,
and though now where
it is redoubled, I am
halved, the day houses it
and my body houses it.

Grace

With movement. A figure moving over grass, a body
moving on what will not move. Over green grass
and among the trees. If a hill comes,
not *if the body approaches a hill*, but, *if a hill comes*,
something is ended.
He said the figure was the figure of a man.
Or, she said, is it in the grass, the still part, the true
on which movement depends, the tree guiding by blocking
the voluptuous body with voluptuousness of its own,
another being physical in the extreme.
She said to be redeemed of this would mean being harmed.
Then he wanted and she wanted it in all places and as often
as possible. In the motion of the figure voluptuous and
restrained as well as in the thin full bodies making up
the still body of the grass. In the hill that approaches and in
the hill moved toward, even in the shapes not spoken of,
the dead who once knew longing, surely,
and still seem to when thought of.

Poem

The white cat's neck is thicker in winter.
It's winter now. Fear also can enlarge her
but not this afternoon. I believe she'll sleep
as I write this like she slept when I thought to write,
when I wanted to pass something through my hand
that would have otherwise remained ideal
or come out my mouth if you were here
or listening. Your mouth is beautiful especially
as its expectation of loss collapses. You remember.
My mouth also was opening.

Confession 7.21.27

Because I see the body of this death, your body,
and know desire for you only through
a remembering that is both intricately close
and far away from me (bright wetness under eyelids
and behind your open mouth), vivid only
in past time, able to do nothing now,
to do nothing more
than be remembered or forgotten,
I hate my will to place you as you are,
undistorted, before me, because I see
your face is nothing like a word
made real by saying, or an object
like the jessamine in rain, tragically
holding itself open, or the rain itself,
itself because it falls. Because I see
that whosoever sees may not so grieve
as if she had not received, I see the body
of this death, my body, made of what it sees.

Her Sleep

One can choose pallor over color at the onset
of an abandonment like sleep. She's most herself
to herself, she's wholly interior, the blank after saturation
which was the moment of her feeling his look on her
as she was falling there, where earlier
he had approached so differently, and was
so differently received. Where she is uncolored
she is herself as much as her arm is, loose
in the bedclothes among the lines making up her hair.
She recedes in order to approach him in this next true way,
as excess of line, as outline, but voiceless, colorless,
shed into him the gold-green and gold-brown
which is his watching her.

His Watching

His relief at being entered exists in him first
as sensation, though earlier he would have said
he would prefer it coming as a good idea
which could be said, and said to her. As it is,
her silence added to his silence makes a corridor
for her inpouring, and he feels tuggings all inside
and leanings which depend on the extravagance
of difference in the body supine on the bed
and his body folded on the bedside chair.
His look keeps ripe his part in the transparency
unstretched by her sleep, where, without thinking
and bodiless, he makes her brush by.

Confession 8.1.2

If I love the dead too much, it's because I heard
from the mouth of Truth there were those who had
made themselves eunuchs for the sake of the kingdom
of heaven. These were the mothers and fathers, O
my God, these were the teachers also, proffering
division in every discipline, on the time lines,
the narrations, the boreal chorales, O the red never
together with the lavender, my God, one language
mundane, one for prayer *pater noster qui es in coelis,*
the more partings the more incorruptible substance
fast in the heart. But my fingers fastened and unfastened
in the hair, at the wrists, high between the legs, or
sometimes at the hard shoulders only with a daughter's love,
and preferred the fastenings. Now that I am given back
the bodies as parcels of ashes, I am come to love ash,
seeing that the grasses never did look back at me,
and the sky wants me small. I love the dead double,
from my body, and because they divide from me.

Heav'n Hides Nothing from Thy View

Will you know also to love me after ending
when presence isn't completely absence yet?
It might be a secrecy like air escaping backward
from the toy or bed you have just blown up
right before insertion of the stopper, something
from your body rushing back to you,
like thoughts of a room you just pull the door on
finally and for the last time, where any action
reeks with privacy, requiring nothing but one mind
resisting mildness but ready to pretend
that memory will do, leaving behind the exact mouth
that surrounded you, and the mother as she recedes,
and the body of the iris bud whose yellow tip
makes you wild.

Taking Pleasure

These new dead leaves are not gathering or resting,
though I would wish it for them, under the evergreen.
There was one thing stained by its reference to us:
a handmade ghost, a decoration, small, tender,
on the far side of the yard beside the hospice . . .

At which point the carver keeps chipping the flint
past utility, making the weapon beautiful.

In the woods, a ruin, a foundation for a house. All around, the bodies
of leaves turn in toward brittleness until the smallest paw
can break them. Someone is walking there, near what was once an edge,
to the apple tree split by the weight of another excellent
unpicked crop. Shudder of presence seeding itself.
Notes, then the bodies of birds punching through.

Who told you that you could eat
that fruit? Why should joy
depend on emptiness?

Scent of ripeness readying the mouth. Touch
following the desire to touch. Before desire, fear of an untouched life.
Before fear, understanding brittleness. Was that you,
coaxed into hunger among the cracking leaves?

The Many Colors

There is a clearing one hopes one is coming to
magically and without accountability but with
grave understanding any minute like a thing
you could see by peeking out the glass in a door:
the raccoon's foreleg moving from the shoulder
slowly in a roundish fear-shape toward the cat-
food bowl, or the adjacent hushed-up feeling of
tenderness one feels flipping through the body
when opening an antique book of photographs
lovingly made of dead stranger children
in a pretty library. They had turned his face
in the direction of the open window he might have
seemed to have suddenly become. The many colors
every day do as much for us as they can.
In the clear place we thought we were meant to be
brought to but not today, a letter came. It said
there was no such thing as mistaken happiness.

Confession 8.9.21

When an open mouth outweighs and outlasts
words, I am a maze of wanderings,
spent arguments, shrinkings. I willed myself
to be made whole, and found will different
from ability. Mind commands the body,
and the body disobeys. Mind commands
the mind and is repelled. Striated iris of the eye
constricts as brightness leaves. Striated iris
in the vase persists in opening. This would be God
not giving me more than I can bear? I think of what
eyes fear to see when held down pleasantly
in sleep, I think of mouths stunned open,
then stunned closed, and I think I would
take heaven by force if, here, where
the flower enters the mirror in the mind
crying *brightness enter me again*, it would be denied
as the soul is denied, by forgetting and remembering,
by wavering, by not being spoken of at all.

Brightness enter me again, odd in proportion,
black duck on brown water, a dark moving
on an utmost heaviness, utmost and outermost
fluttering the body of the inmost pond. Desire invents
as loss invents, stationed in endings or beginnings,
urged by their own weights to seek their places,
and every body heavy. Can I become a girl again
if I perceive myself a girl? If I was a child,
I also was a darkness before that, relic I bear about me
in my body, palpable now because of love, and because
of loss of love. Brightness, be an instrument against
the floral changes too slight in the mind, the feminine
too attentive of being seen. Revisit the inmost
shapes that opposites create by arcing toward, find
the small place heavy with a prior deathlessness,
an interior that skin can mark the outer boundary of.
Enter me there, and inside there, where love
remains unfixed and questions every answer.

Notes

The poems titled "Confession" derive language from the *Confessions of St. Augustine*, translated by E. B. Pusey. The numbers in the titles of these poems refer to passages from Pusey's translation.

"Nude against the Light" is after a painting of the same name by Bonnard.

"Thimble Forest" and "Homage to the Romantic Ballet" are also titles of constructions by Joseph Cornell.

"Dyke Breach" is also the title of a painting by Karl Schmidt-Rottluff.

"Pietà" begins and ends with phrases from Julia Kristeva's *Black Sun: Depression and Melancholia*.

"Confession 9.10.25" is for Daryl Lofdahl.

"Five-Part Question" has its form partly derived from the medieval Serbian poem "The Message of King Sakis and the Legend of the Twelve Dreams He Had in One Night."

"Personae Separatae" is also the title of a poem by Eugenio Montale.

"Grace" is for Matthew Harvey.

The poems "Her Sleep" and "His Watching" are after Picasso's *Meditation (Contemplation)*.

1987
Elton Glaser, *Tropical Depressions*
Michael Pettit, *Cardinal Points*

1988
Bill Knott, *Outremer*
Mary Ruefle, *The Adamant*

1989
Conrad Hilberry, *Sorting the Smoke*
Terese Svoboda, *Laughing Africa*

1990
Philip Dacey,
    Night Shift at the Crucifix Factory
Lynda Hull, *Star Ledger*

1991
Greg Pape, *Sunflower Facing the Sun*
Walter Pavlich,
    Running near the End of the World

1992
Lola Haskins, *Hunger*
Katherine Soniat, *A Shared Life*

1993
Tom Andrews,
    The Hemophiliac's Motorcycle
Michael Heffernan, *Love's Answer*
John Wood, *In Primary Light*

1994
James McKean, *Tree of Heaven*
Bin Ramke, *Massacre of the Innocents*
Ed Roberson,
    Voices Cast Out to Talk Us In

1995
Ralph Burns, *Swamp Candles*
Maureen Seaton, *Furious Cooking*

1996
Pamela Alexander, *Inland*
Gary Gildner,
    The Bunker in the Parsley Fields
John Wood,
    The Gates of the Elect Kingdom

1997
Brendan Galvin, *Hotel Malabar*
Leslie Ullman, *Slow Work through Sand*

1998
Kathleen Peirce, *The Oval Hour*
Bin Ramke, *Wake*
Cole Swensen, *Try*